WE WIN:

A Father's Journey Through Autism

MR. KRIS SHINN

TABLE OF CONTENTS

INTRODUCTION

Strength. I have had the blessing of knowing Kris Shinn for 24 years, and in that time strength has always been the word that best describes him. When I met Kris, he was enduring intense training every day in the weight room and on the track. His dedication and hard work led him to All-American status in the shot putt. I once watched him bench-press 500 pounds. There was also the time that he moved my washing machine… by himself. The physical strength that Kris possessed when I met him, while impressive, would not be the strength that I would come to admire most.

When Kris called to tell me his son, Will, had just been diagnosed with autism, for the first time in our friendship, I was at a loss for words. The thing I did know, was that the strongest person I knew, had just been brought to his knees. As he soon learned, that was the perfect place to start... on his knees. God had a plan for Kris and for Will that no one could fathom.

I am in awe of the strength I now see in my friend Kris. His ability to share all the struggles and successes of having a son with autism is truly inspiring. I know it is hard for him to relive a lot of the hard times he and Will have faced, but Kris knows that by sharing, he might make someone else's struggle a little easier. God's plan is being revealed more and more each day. This book is part of that plan. I believe, without a doubt, God chose Kris and his unwavering strength to help lift others in their time of need so that they might come to know Him.

– Chad Brinkley

"Iron sharpeneth iron, so a man sharpeneth the countenance of his friend." -Proverbs 27:17

FORWARD

I met Kris several years ago in a crisis management course I teach. He wanted to learn how to safely control his own son (Will) and how to prevent him from going into crisis. More than this, however, Kris wanted to teach other parents how to safely manage their own children with special needs. As I got to know him a little bit better I realized that he was a pretty special kind of guy. Kris is the kind of person who can take some good information and run with it, using that information to help himself, and more importantly help others. This book will provide the parents of children with special needs with some insights, laughs, tears, and some stories of the joy of learning to meet the challenges of raising children with autism and/or related disabilities. This book, however, isn't just for parents of special needs kids, it's also for people like me who wish to understand (at least a bit better) *what life is like for the parents of children with special needs*. Kris explains his own journey with a combination of humor, insight, love, common-sense and most of all his own faith.

The book takes the reader through the various stages of living with a child with special needs including the shock of an early diagnosis and a gloomy prognosis for the future. Kris talks about some of the day to day challenges, working with schools, the value of a supportive community, family, and religion and how he himself has been transformed not only into a better parent, but also into a better person. Although shaken at first, to his core, Kris now has a positive attitude towards the challenges that he, his family and Will are now facing and those that they will encounter in the future. Speaking as someone who is looking in from the outside, it seems that having a special needs child (like any great challenge) can either beat you down or make you stronger. Kris has chosen the latter, but he also makes it clear that meeting these challenges isn't simple nor easy, but nothing worth doing ever is. Kris has a clear view of the future for his son and that involves preparing him for life as a functioning member of society to the greatest extent possible. To quote one of my favorite passages, "He (Will) has so many more abilities than he has disabilities as we see it. The issue is figuring out how to get those (skills) out of him in a way that he can utilize them for his future." I believe that all readers will find the book insightful and inspiring and that those with children/family members with disabilities will take comfort in knowing that they're not alone and they will also find some strategies to help them cope with the never-ending challenges they face. The rest of us, who may not face these challenges directly, but (like myself) work with parents to overcome these challenges, can gain a bit more insight into the lives of families with special needs children.

Merrill Winston, Ph.D., BCBA-D

CH1 MY CAREER

I had just finished with throwing the discus at the conference meet at Harding University in Searcy, AR. It was my freshman year at Ouachita Baptist University. I look up and here he comes my dad. "So, are you ready to come home now?" he says to me. "No way, no how am I leaving!" I said. What my dad was referring to was a something he and I had discussed the previous semester. My dad had made this statement to me, "If you want to move home after track season is over, then that will be ok." You see he was much smarter than me, and he knew me so well. After the competition there was no way I would leave.

I made a decision to attend Ouachita Baptist University earlier in the spring while I was in high school in Marshall, Texas. I had received numerous letters from several colleges that wanted me to come visit and see what they had to offer. I had done really well in track for the last several years throwing the shot put and discus. My parents and I were very hopeful that it would help pay for or pay for my college education. I went to visit with Dr. Bob Gravett, who was the track coach at OBU, on a Saturday morning in early April. After eating at Mrs. T's that morning, a hot spot in Arkadelphia, AR, he took me down to the track facilities and showed me around. I was pretty impressed with what OBU had to offer as well as the very nice campus they had. I told Coach Gravett that I would have to go home and discuss this further with my parents and also consider some of the other schools that wanted me to visit. He told me he would help pay for my school if I was interested in being a part of the team. We shook hands and I was back on my way home. That was the beginning of my stay in Arkadelphia and at OBU. Little did I know at the time that I was about to embark on one of the most rewarding but toughest times of my life.

A couple weeks later, I sent my letter of intent to Coach Gravett, and my career at OBU would begin in the fall. My first semester was one of the most difficult times of my life up to that time. I had never been away from my parents for very long at all, but was close to the extended family that lived just twenty-five minutes away. I suffered from horrible headaches and was very fortunate to be eligible in the spring semester considering how terrible my first semester had been. I didn't eat in the cafeteria much nor come out of my room much except for class and track practice. Needless to say, I was a bit home-sick, even traveling the twenty five minutes every weekend to my aunt and uncle's. I called my parents a lot during that first semester wanting to come home. My dad would often get on the phone with me after I am sure I upset my mom. He would talk me through whatever it was I was going through at the time and has continued to do so. God knew I would need a strong set of parents, and He definitely blessed me with the best!

I think it was somewhere around Thanksgiving that my dad made the statement to me about "coming home" after track season was over the next semester. Looking back, I know he knew there was no way I would after I got to compete because I was so busy the spring semester that I had no time to think about much other than school and track. It turned out exactly like he had hoped it would when I told him at the conference meet "there is no way I am leaving". I had just won the conference cham-pionship as a freshman in the discus. I was on cloud nine! I think the truth be told my parents were as well, and I am really sure my dad breathed a sigh of relief. Despite the difficulties I experienced that first year of college, I learned a lot about myself and the person I would become.

That was just the beginning of my career at OBU. My sophomore year was not quite as good. I bombed out at the conference meet and finished fifth in both events. I did, however, compete at the National Track meet in Stephenville, Texas, that spring and finished in the top fifteen in the discus. I believed it was a really good sign for the things to come. Good things for me personally and for my career at OBU.

During my junior year, the fall semester brought a sense of a new phase in my athletic career. I started a job as the student assistant manager of the HYPER Building on campus. A job which allowed me more time to work out and train since most of the facilities were housed in that building. In my role as student assistant manager, I was also able to facilitate the introduction of an indoor shot put ring allowing me to practice all year round despite the weather. I started the spring semester with a great sense of accomplishment. My continual practice had yielded new distances I had never reached before. School was going great and I was on track to graduate the next spring. I was finding success in the indoor meets. I won at the conference meet and had a qualifying distance which qualified me for the National Association of Intercollegiate Athletics (NAIA) indoor meet held in Kansas City, Missouri.

After training diligently for weeks, the day finally arrived to leave for the Kansas City meet. I was a little intimidated when my teammates and I walked into the arena where we were to compete. Saturday morning came early, and it was my time to compete on the national arena. I was in the second flight of throwers in the shot put. I warmed up with great intensity hoping to do my best. As I stepped up for my turn and I saw my parents on the upper deck right cheering me on I knew "it was my time". My dad looked at me and said, "You can do this!" And I did...I finished fourth that day making *All American* for the first time. My parents were filled with excitement and pride. It was a great day for all of us, and one I will never forget.

Competing in both indoor and outdoor meets, I continued to train. I found success in the outdoor season as well. At the conference meet at Harding University in Searcy, Arkansas, I was the first male athlete to win the indoor shot, outdoor shot and the discus all in the same season in the history of our conference which qualified me for the national outdoor meet. The National Association of Intercollegiate Athletics (NAIA) outdoor meet was held in Vancouver, British Columbia. I finished fourth for shot put and in the top ten for discus earning me another *All American* honor that year. It was a great time in my life, full of accomplishment, pride, and success.

My senior year started out by having a scope down on my right knee; however the prognosis for my spring senior season was still good with surgery taking place so soon in the school year. Recovery went well, and I was ready to go when spring arrived. I won the indoor conference meet with a career best 55' throw winning the event by 12'. Qualifying once again for the NAIA indoor meet, I was headed to Kansas City, Missouri in two weeks. Entering the meet, I had the second farthest qualifying throw in the country. Unfortunately, things didn't go so well for me that week. I finished seventh by three inches, three inches from making All American. The winning throw was 55'2". Only 2" farther than I had thrown just two weeks earlier. Although disappointed, I held my head high because I still had the outdoor season left to go.

The outdoor season started with a bang. I qualified for Nationals my first meet of the season. However, the outdoor season didn't come without complications. Easter weekend I was hospitalized with kidney stones, missing several days of school and training. Luckily, it didn't affect the conference meet. I was successfully able to compete, winning both the shot put and discus, giving me three individual titles once again in two consecutive years. At the end of the spring semester, OBU has a sports banquet for all athletes in all sports. The evening always included lots of laughter and jokes, success stories, and awards for each sport. The highest award for the evening was the OBU Athlete of the year. This award was selected by the coaches of every sport. What an honor it was for me to be selected as the Ouachita Baptist University Athlete of the Year. As an athlete, I had trained with and cheered on many of the athletes during my four years. So I knew what great athletes there were to choose from. I humbly accepted the award. It is to this day the greatest award I have ever received and one I will always cherish from my track career.

In closing out my senior year, I was once again headed to Vancouver for the national track meet, although I had graduated two weeks prior with my BA in Business Administration. I competed well, but finished seventh in the shot put and ninth in the discus putting an end to my track and field days. My career at Ouachita Baptist University as a student and now athlete was over! My time at college ended up being a great time in my life. I was so blessed to be able to participate in athletics and compete while getting my education at the same time. I am so thankful my dad made that deal with me. He was glad he was right and so am I! Looking back at it all now, I know my experiences at Ouachita helped to prepare me for those things that were to come...

CH 2 THAT DREADED DAY

O n a bright sunny April day in 2003 as I traveled alone to Little Rock, Arkansas, to Children's Hospital, I was meeting my ex-wife and my son, Will, at The Dennis Developmental Center for some testing. A few months earlier we had divorced, and she and my three children had moved about two hours north of me. The winter had been rough for me, and unbeknownst to everyone, it was about to get rougher than I could have ever imagined. As I pulled into the center, parking places were surprisingly abundant; I happily chose one that would allow me an easy departure after our appointment to get back to work.

I sat anxiously waiting in my car for them to arrive. I was looking forward to seeing Will, yet wondering how the appointment would go. He was two and a half years old and since the separation, I only saw him every three weeks at my house. Upon arrival, he seemed to be in a pretty good mood, although his mom and I were a bundle of nerves about the appointment and feeling awkward as we attempted to present a united front. In September 2002, Will had been referred to the center by an audiologist after administering several hearing tests. We had suspected that he had a hearing problem because he was not talking, failed to look at us when we talked to him, and didn't seem like he understood what we were saying when we talked to him. Surprisingly to us, the audiologist did not find any significant problems with Will's hearing. He told us that we probably needed to get an appointment at The Dennis Developmental Center to get him "checked out". (Wow, I didn't know what that would mean at the time!) We took his recommendation and made an appointment, having no clue as to what it was for, what it meant, or how it would change our lives forever.

We gathered all the items we thought Will might need for the day and headed into the center to check him in for his appointment. The three of us sat in the waiting room for what seemed like forever, although I am certain it was probably only several minutes. A nice young lady came to the waiting area to get Will. She began to explain to us that they would be conducting a full battery of test on him taking up most of the day. She continued to explain that we would not be allowed to see the majority of the testing or allowed to be with him during the evaluation. Understandably, we were upset by this information; neither my ex-wife nor I felt comfortable leaving Will not knowing what they were going to do with him, nor by the fact that it left us together to wait. The seconds seemed like minutes and minutes like hours as the morning went by. I could hear him occasionally yell out, making sounds like I had often heard him do at home. Hearing those sounds coming from behind closed doors with the inability to know what was happening made the morning very tough for the both of us.

Finally the morning testing session was complete. They returned Will to us. Although he looked frustrated as he quite often did; he appeared okay. We were released to go to lunch and told to return within an hour. In our efforts to keep Will happy, we took him to his favorite restaurant....McDonalds! Upon arriving at McDonald's he was a very happy little camper. He was getting to do one of his favorite things....EAT!

23

Despite his eagerness to eat, I wasn't that hungry. I was too concerned about him, worried about what had taken place that morning, and dreading what was yet to come in the afternoon testing. Of course our hour quickly passed, and it was time to head back. We arrived at the center, and Will became increasingly agitated as he realized we were going back again. Thankfully we were able to calm him down, assuring him it was okay and that we were going too.

We entered the center, sat, and waited. The nice young lady returned to get Will. This time we were allowed to follow behind keeping ourselves hidden from Will so we could watch. He was in an enclosed room with a lot of cool stuff to play with. At times someone would be in there with him and at others he was left alone. As a dad watching from the outside, I found it to be very interesting, yet scary and a little overwhelming all rolled up into the same breath for me. I had very little understanding of what they were doing or trying to do but sure wasn't going to ask anyone either. In what felt like only seconds of watching, we were asked to return to the waiting room until he was done.

Feeling like an eternity we waited... I am not the most patient person on any given day, but at that particular time in my life, I was even worse. The hours seemed like days. The longer we waited the more anxious and impatient I became. We continued to hear Will behind the closed doors yell and scream. I recognized it as the sounds of a little boy who was mad! And mad he surely was! Here I was sitting, doing nothing in this waiting room yet feeling like my child needed me. It was tough! As his daddy, I wanted to rush in and help him, calm him down, or beat someone up for making him mad. He was just a little boy. But I knew I shouldn't interfere with what they were doing or the testing that was occurring. Needless to say, it was a very long afternoon!

Our wait was over finally. The lady returned and asked us to follow her to the meeting room. Upon entering, several adults and Will were already there waiting. Although overwhelmed with the number of adults in the room, we were excited to finally see Will and he us. The adults began introductions, although I didn't really catch names, it was a doctor and several therapists which increased my nervousness as what lied ahead. As Will played in the floor, they began to tell us what they had done as far as testing Will. They spoke using large terms, most of which I had never heard before, and sure didn't really understand. They continued to talk on and on as I sat dazedly trying to pay attention to the words, make sense of what they were saying while focusing on Will. After what seemed like forever, the doctor turned and looked at me and said, *"Do you have any questions?"* Thinking to myself, now you want to know if I have questions? I haven't understood most of what you have said. With all the strength I could muster, I said *"Most of what you have told us today doesn't make a lot of sense to me. You haven't really told us what is wrong or what we can do. Can you please tell me what is wrong with my child?"* You know, we all have times in our lives we look back on and wish some words had never come out of our mouths. Those words are mine. The words I spoke that day have rung in my ears pretty much every day since April of 2003. Little did I know at that time, that what the doctor was about to say would change the course of our lives forever.

*"**Mr. Shinn, your son has moderate to severe autism. He may never be able to speak and will most likely have to be put in an institution by the time he is 12**,"* said the doctor. There was complete and utter silence that followed the words that just came from her mouth. I was speechless and in shock. We just stood there, in an attempt to break the deafening silence. The doctor asked if we had any questions. Thinking I must have surely misunderstood what she had said, I asked her to repeat it. I needed to have the

opportunity to hear her correctly. Again she stated, *"Mr. Shinn, your son has moderate to severe autism. He may never be able to speak and will most likely have to be put in an institution by the time he is 12,"* I sat in shock as I watched my son play in the floor. I was overwhelmed with emotion, disbelief, confusion, and anger. It all began to overwhelm me as I just sat there, not really knowing what to say, what to ask, or how to feel. They continued to talk, yet all they had left to say to us was you need to get him into therapy as soon as you can and good luck. That's it? Good luck? Therapies? We gathered up our things trying to hold ourselves together and our emotions in for Will. We didn't want him to know anything was wrong. How little we knew at that time. Knowing now what we do, Will probably already knew himself!

We walked to the vehicle in silence; I told them bye and that I would be in touch as soon as possible. As I reached the safety of my car, I could no longer control my emotions. I got into my car and begin to weep bitterly for almost two hours. My mother and best friend called to check on the day's events, but although I tried to talk, but words just wouldn't come. All I could seem to do was cry. I was so overcome with my emotions, my behavior frightened my mother. Being unable to speak and only cry into the phone, I was unable to even tell her what the doctor had said was wrong with Will.

Eventually after crying, screaming, and praying, I begin to calm down. I had regained control of my emotions enough that I was able to call my mom. Although I am not confident of exactly what I said to her, I do remember what one thing was she said to me. *"Kris, I am not sure what we will do or can do, but whatever it is we will do it together."* Later that evening, I talked to my best friend. As any good friend would do, he made me feel better. Although at that time neither of us had any idea of what lay ahead.

Despite the encouragement from my parents and my friend, all I could think is, "How can I do this?" After going through a divorce, my kids moving two hours away, and now this, I felt I truly reached up to touch the bottom. I had no hope. I truly thought that it was over for me. How would I ever be able to handle all of this and survive?

CH3 ARE THEY JUST WORDS

S ome days, time seemed to fly by while others seemed to stand still for long periods of time. The months following Will's diagnosis of autism seemed like a blur yet others seemed like a forever journey. The therapies started, the medications were given, and the sleep ended while dealing with the symptoms of this thing called autism. I really wanted to bury my head in the sand and just pretend my world wasn't falling down around me, and at times I still do. It seemed easier to deal with everything by not dealing with anything at all. However, when I finally came out of the sand guess what? The problems were still there, and not only were they still there, but they had compounded themselves. If there was only one thing I could tell you about receiving an autism diagnosis or any diagnosis is this...DO NOT BURY YOUR HEAD IN THE SAND...

There is an old saying, *"Time heals all wounds."* That is a flat out lie. Time doesn't heal anything. It may give you the added strength to carry on, but it does not heal anything; only God heals all wounds, and then only **IF** we will let him. I have had and continue to have a lot of wounds that I desperately needed God to heal, some of those are in the following paragraphs.

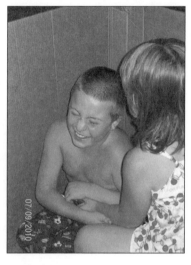

Blame... Blame is a word and a feeling that is used way too much in a lot of wrong places. I blamed myself for years for autism being in Will's life. I just knew it was my fault, and I was bound and determined to *"fix"* it. Well, after years of trying, it is still not fixed! I am not saying it hasn't improved, but at the end of the day, Will still has autism. Autism is not something that any one human can fix. We can take him to all kinds of therapies, but there is no fix or miracle pill available. The only *One* who can fix it is God, if He so chooses. I have faith that he may well choose to do so in His time. In the meantime, I will occupy till He comes!

Regret ... An emotion that closely follows blame. Many of us who play the blame game look back in the past with regret. We revisit and become self-accusers of things we couldn't or didn't do more of, or things we did and shouldn't have. We continue to blame ourselves over and over. *"I should have known,"* is what I kept telling myself, but how could I have known in 2003?? There wasn't much on the internet at that time. The incidence of autism was on the rise but not like it is today. I look back at that time in my life now, and I am filled with regret that I didn't do more. But the biggest problem with regret is that it causes me not to do more now as well. It creeps in like a virus, and eventually it will eat you up.

Helplessness... I wanted to fix it, like all dads we are supposed to fix things that go wrong for our children. But with this, there was no fix. I felt so helpless. I couldn't help my own child through this because I had no idea what to do. I have found that there aren't too many things worse in this world than for a man, the leader of his household, to feel helpless. But, I am here to tell you that with God *all things are possible*. You are not helpless. He empowers you to do what you need to do, puts you in places you need to be, and loves you the entire way.

Alone... As I walked this path as many parents do, I felt ultimately alone much of the time. I questioned myself constantly wondering if I was the only one who knows how this is. How could God leave me when I needed Him the most? But over the years, I have come to realize that he hasn't gone anywhere. He knew this was to happen before I ever faced that life changing day in April so many years ago. Things happen in this life for a reason, and I am confident that God will use me in every situation good or bad if I will allow him to. It has taken me years to recognize that although at times I feel as though I am alone in my pain and isolation, I am not. God said, he would never leave me or forsake me, and at those times I had to continually tell myself, *"You are not alone!"* Some days I listened and others I didn't. I have been to the depths of that road when I reached up just to touch bottom. It is a desperate and very lonely place to be. God never intended for me to be in that place, but I allowed myself to go there and sometimes stay for a while. Thankfully God He never gives up on us, never walks away, and never throws away the clay but continually works at making us into a new creation!

Anger... One of the most destructive stages I experience. I wish I could say that in past tense, but there are days even now that I find myself revisiting this stage. I was mad at God. I was mad at myself. I was mad at my ex-wife. I was mad at the world. I took out my frustration on everyone and everything; it didn't matter to me that they had nothing to do with it. I can now see that much of my anger was a result of my life not turning out how I had envisioned it to be; but praise God it hasn't. Today, I am getting to do things and help countless numbers of people because of my experiences. God saw the big picture. I am convinced that he brought me through that time of my life in order to use me now. Preparation for some tasks isn't easy, and some days I wonder what God was thinking. But, I have learned to turn my anger into trust believing he has a plan.

Frustration... As adults we often find ourselves in situations that we "want" to control, but for reasons outside of our control, we can't. Autism is one of those situations. During that time of our lives, I often got frustrated with Will. His constant screaming, unruly behavior, and temper tantrums led me to the highest level of frustration possible. I didn't understand what was wrong, how to help, or what to do. After all of these years, I see that he was doing the best he could at the time, and all he was asking me to do was step up my game too. I cannot imagine the frustration he feels on a daily basis. Although the frustration levels have lessened in severity, they will never end. Families with children on the spectrum have struggles in many areas of life. But, I have found that some frustration is good; it stretches us to new heights and new ways of doing things. One thing I know for sure is that despite the frustration we as parents or adults may feel, it is nothing compared to that of my son and the many other children with disabilities living in a world that quite frankly is not up to their standards.

Pity... During this time, I often found myself in the middle of the self-pity pool. I felt sorry for myself. Why didn't I get the white picket fence, the 2.5 kids and the two story house like I saw on TV as I was growing up? I was having to accept the hard reality that my life would never be the way it was when I was a child. My son's life would never be what I had envisioned for him. His siblings were not getting the life I had envisioned for them, either. I found myself feeling sorry for all of us. I just wanted to stick all of our heads back in the sand hoping this time it would work. Nope! It didn't work then, and it won't work now. Pity, self-inflicted or bestowed on others, never works well for anyone. It only produces blame, frustration, and other vile parts of this journey that kept us from going where we needed to be.

Denial... It's not a river! For quite some time, I wanted to believe that what I had been told about Will was wrong. I did not want to face the reality of it; I hoped that if I didn't acknowledge it, it wasn't true. But the ugly truth about denial is that it doesn't do anyone any favors. It only prolongs the inevitable and delays what could have been help for my child; the child who didn't ask for this, who didn't deserve this, and can't help himself. In the history of denial, no one has ever benefited from being in denial! In today's technology based society, there is so much information readily available that no parent has an excuse for living in denial. In my experience in speaking with families, I have seen how difficult it is for most fathers to accept that there is a problem with their child. I have seen that I am not the only one that was in denial that they could not *"fix"* their child. As males, we are trained early in life to be strong, be dependable, and be a fixer. That's what we do; as sons, brothers, husbands, and dads. But for Autism, there is no fix, there is no magic pill, there is no cure. There is however a wide variety of therapies, medications, special diets, interventions and teaching methods that can help our children be the best they can be. Get out of denial; it is time for you to do what you do best. Be strong, be dependable, and be a fixer by doing right by your child and for your child.

Forgiveness... I was in such a twisted and struggling place that I had to really pull myself up by the boot straps and figure out how to forgive myself. In this life, most people need to forgive themselves more than anyone, and most of the time you are the person hardest for you to forgive. If I forgive myself then I really can't blame myself anymore, and without that, it takes away my need to roll around in all my self-pity. Forgiveness is not easy; it is a struggle in every way. When we begin to forgive ourselves, we begin to lose all the issues we have been drowning ourselves in for months or maybe even years as to not have to deal with the issues at hand. Forgive yourself for whatever it is you have been carrying all this time. Ask God to forgive you for trying to carry the load for which he intended for you to hand to Him anyway. God loves you, and I promise you He is just waiting on you.

The Bible says in Romans 8:28, *"And we know that all things work together for good to them that love God, to them who are called according to his purpose."* All of the things I have mentioned in the paragraphs preceding have nothing to do with His purpose, but He uses them to get you to your purpose through Him. Do I have regrets....*yes!* Do I still blame myself at times.....*yes!* Do I get still get frustrated at times....*yes!* Do I live in denial at times..... *maybe!* Do I get angry at times....*for sure!* But am I able to forgive myself when all those things creep up......*yes!* Sometimes it may take help from others to do so, but I have realized that I am not alone unless I choose to be. The life as a family with a child with autism is a life that requires a village. We truly need each other, becoming isolated from the world or each other is not productive. The world will isolate us enough without our help or those around us! Fight the good fight and stay the course. Our kids are worth it!

CH. 4 MY HELP

It was a good 'ole hot August day in 2003, and I was playing a practice round of golf with a friend in preparation for a golf tournament in Memphis, Tennessee. We had played several holes that afternoon when I got the call. Although engaged in my game, I realized the call was from brother's house in Mississippi. Alarmed, I answered the phone. My brother, who is several years older than I, began to tell me about our maternal grandmother. Granny had been in an accident in our hometown of Malvern. He explained that she had been rushed to the hospital and that she might not make it through night. Being several hours away, he told me stay put for now and he would keep me posted. Unable to concentrate on the game with thoughts of my family flooding my mind, the afternoon was somewhat of a blur. Later that evening, he called to notify me of my granny's

passing. She had just celebrated her 83rd birthday the day before. Although overwhelmed with my own sadness, I called my mom knowing she would not be doing well. Still hours away from home, she wanted me to wait until morning to make the trip.

I woke up early that Saturday morning and headed towards my hometown. My parents lived in south Arkansas and were staying with family. After hugs and hellos were shared, I begin to ask questions about what had caused the accident. My mom begin to explain how my granny had been in a shopping center in front of a very busy stretch of highway which consisted of five lanes. Granny, apparently blinded by the bright afternoon sun, pulled out in front of a Dooley hauling a fifth wheel. The driver couldn't stop in time, despite his effort, and crashed into the driver's side of my granny's car. Unbeknownst to me, the events surrounding the accident would forever change my life. Granny didn't make it, but I think she would be pleased with the outcome surrounding her death.

As my mom continued the story, she began to tell me about "that girl", the one who had gotten out of her car from Sonic to help my granny. "That girl" she stated, had rushed to see if Granny was ok and called 911. Granny asked her to look in her purse to find the number of her daughter, my mom's youngest sister. Finding the number, she made the call to my aunt alerting her of the accident. The ambulance arrived and took my Granny to the nearest hospital as "that girl" followed them. My family quickly arrived at the hospital to check on Granny where they learned the details of the accident and the status of her injuries. My mom continued to share how they had met "that girl" in the waiting area and how awesome it was that someone had actually got involved in something they didn't have to be involved in...just to help another human being. Knowing that someone was with Granny during such a scary time seemed to bring her peace as it did the rest of our family. As she continued to weep, she told me that Granny's injuries were just too severe and that she was not able to overcome them.

Later in the day, my parents and I went to the funeral home to assist the family in making arrangements for the services. The visitation was set for the upcoming Monday night and the graveside service following on Tuesday afternoon. My brother, a pastor, would be conducting the services. I stayed throughout the day with my family talking and eating like families do when they are together. Family members gathered that hadn't seen each other in years, and it saddened me that it takes events such as a death to draw all of us together from our daily lives.

Monday arrived and I returned to Malvern for my granny's visitation. I stood across from the entrance in order to observe everyone entering to view Granny and give condolences to my family. Being a people watcher helped me from becoming overwhelmed with sadness and gave me something to do. As with any visitation, people poured in, many of whom I didn't recognize and some I surely didn't know. As I was taking count of those who walked in, this one young lady caught my eye. I was quite certain I didn't know her. I quickly made my way over to my mom asking who that lady was. I begin to hear how she was "that girl". "That girl" whom I had heard about only days ago. "That girl" who helped my granny, and "that girl" had a name, and it was Brandi.

My mom, noticing I was smitten, motioned for her to come over where we were standing and she introduced me to her. She was very beautiful, but I could tell she had been crying. She told me she felt so bad for us and that she wished she could have done more to help. I told her thanks. She did a lot more than most people would have done to help. My mom took her into the room to see the rest of my family, and I began to visit with others where I was standing. As she came out, I told her again how much I appreciated what she had done to help. The night went on with a lot of people coming in and visiting with all of us. Granny would have been upset over the "fuss" that she was getting. She was great lady, and she is still missed to this day. She loved her garden and her family!

The next morning arrived and I had been up early to get ready to drive back for the funeral. You may be wondering why I didn't just stay the night in Malvern. Well, at that time there were only two things that I had left from my life before my divorce and the diagnosis for Will, my car and my house. I couldn't sleep anywhere else and frankly didn't even want to try. So,

I got ready and drove down to meet my parents at the church where we were to have lunch after the service. My parents, brother, and I all rode to the service together. My brother was the only one of his family that could come and my kids were too young to bring.

Ken did an amazing job as he always does. My granny was now laid to rest right beside Papaw and my brother made reference to the legacy they left behind which was their family. After the service, I noticed Brandi, "that girl", was there and she had someone else with her. My dad asked me to go get the car which was on the other side of the cemetery. I went to get the car and drove around to pick up my family and there stood Brandi and this other lady. I stopped by where they were and rolled down my window to speak to them. My mom was already talking to them once I got there. My dad and brother were getting into the car, and I told her how much I appreciated her again and thanked her. She introduced the other lady there, and it was her mother who had come with her. My mom got into the car and I began to drive away. My brother, of all people, pipes up from the back and says, "You know she is kind of cute. We should have asked more about her." Then my dad pipes up and says, "We sure should have!" My mother joins in and says, "Hey, stop the car, and we will just do that." You have to know that my dad would do something like that, but for my mom and brother to jump in was something out of the ordinary. I told them all to hush it; we were at a funeral and I was hungry. They all just laughed as we drove away to the church to have some lunch.

We sat down and had a nice lunch with all my mom's family at the church I grew up in as a child. It had changed a lot but still had the same feel, like home. I sure needed that at the time and was grateful for sure. I finished my lunch and was ready to go back to my house for the rest of the day and start work again on Wednesday. As I was telling my mom goodbye and ready to head out the door, something came over me and I said, "Mom, if you talk to her find out more about her." I was referring to Brandi. My mom politely said she would. I left and drove home ready to be back in my comfort zone.

Several days passed and I was trying to get back into my normal routine, if you can call it that! It was about 7pm Thursday night and my cell phone rang. I looked at it and it was my mom calling me. I answered and we talked for several minutes asking how everyone was doing and how she was doing. My mom checked on me a lot during that time because she knew I had been through a very rough time. Then she asked me what I wanted her to find out and/or tell Brandi. At first I wasn't sure who she was referring to and asked what she meant. She reminded me that I had asked her to find out more about her when I left the church on Tuesday, and she was going to call her that night. I remembered that and I told her to tell her I was divorced, had three kids and one had severe autism. She said that she would. We said our goodbyes and she hung up. I thought nothing more about it because that information would scare off anyone I knew for sure.

I went about my business the rest of the evening and about 8pm my phone rang again. It was my mom... again. (Please, don't tell her I said that.) Anyway, I answered the phone, and she began to tell me she had been talking to Brandi, and that she and Brandi had discussed me and what I had told my mom to tell her about me. Well, Brandi wanted my mom to give me her number. She also wanted me to know she was divorced, had five dogs and was a Special Education Teacher. I was in shock to say the least. I wrote her number down, and we finished our conversation and hung up. I really didn't give it a whole lot of thought for about thirty minutes or so. I went back by my chair and saw the paper with her number on it and my gut said to call her. My head said "You are nuts." They battle like that often, but the gut usually wins out because that is the Spirit talking to me. I like Him!

I sat down in my chair and started to dial the number. It was around 9 pm at this time. I heard her voice say hello on the other end of the line, and we began to talk. Her biggest questions were "Why me? Why am I involved in this?" We talked about all of it for about an hour. You have to understand that I was not a big phone talker at all. I would rather talk in person than on a phone, so this was pretty excessive for me, and I think it was for her at the time as well. It was almost 10 pm and I asked her if she might like to meet me in Little Rock the next night for dinner so we could talk more. I didn't really like the phone remember? She told me that it was all too fresh and that would be kind of weird for her having dinner with the grandson of the woman she tried to help who had passed away a week before this. I told her I understood, and we talked some more.

This call rocked on for another two hours, we had been on the phone since 9 pm and it was now midnight. She asked, "Can I change my mind?" I then asked her, "About what?" She said, "About meeting you tomorrow night?" I said, "Sure!" Then she asked me to meet her at Olive Garden in Little Rock for dinner at 7 pm. We talked for another hour after that till 1 am. We had been on the phone talking for four hours straight. My hand and ear were about to fall off from being on the phone so long, but it was the best conversation I had had in a long time. Finally, I told her I had to go because I had to be at work early that Friday since we were moving our office. She reluctantly let me go and we said we would see each other at seven the next evening.

I was dragging the following morning and my office just about killed me. We were moving all that stuff to our new offices. One of my coworkers asked me why I was dragging and I told her what had gone on the night before. She told me she had a feeling something good was up because I had a different expression on my face that day. I said that was because I was tired, and she was working me like a dog!

I got home and began to get ready for my dinner that evening. I arrived at Olive Garden about 6:40 as I am not late anywhere 99.9% of the time. I was there waiting when she arrived. She was more beautiful than I remembered, and her smile captivated me immediately. We shook hands and went into the restaurant. We had a great meal and great conversation. She had on a lot of jewelry, and it was all so coordinated and I was fascinated. We sat at the table for a long time and realized they needed it for other people so we decided to go see a movie.

We began to talk even more about our lives and where we had been and wanted to go. It became more apparent to me as we spent more time together that God had set this up with the help of my Granny. The movie was really good, but the company was unmatched. Yes, sitting in the movie that night we did discuss getting married, where we would live, and a lot of different stuff that doesn't usually come up- or shouldn't- on a first date. We then left the movie and went back to Olive Garden to get her car so she could go home. We sat in my car for a longtime talking about everything under the sun it seems now. We even had a police officer knock on my window, about scaring both of us half to death, wanting to know if we were alright. We left there about 3 am and went our separate ways. That week changed my life forever.

If you know anything about us, Brandi Garret is now Brandi Shinn. Ever since that night in Little Rock we have been together. We got married about ten months later and have been married for over ten years now. Does Granny know that she helped change lives that fateful day for her in August of 2003? I am sure God has let her know. This is how I met my wife, mother to Will and bonus mother to my girls.

Here is a little about her that you will find interesting, I assure you.

We are the same age (very young).

She is the oldest of seven children (1 biological sister and five adopted siblings).

Her parents were Therapeutic Foster Parents for many years.

She has a Special Ed Degree.

She has a Master's Degree.

She has a Graduate Certificate Degree in Autism Spectrum Disorder.

She taught Special Ed for 10+ years.

She has a sister who is a Special Ed Teacher.

She has a family member with autism.
She has the biggest heart God could have given anyone!

You see, I couldn't have scripted all this any better, or even asked for any more than God had planned for me and my kids. He knew before I was born what we needed, and it was "that girl", our Brandi!

CH5 IT TAKES A VILLAGE

In the last chapter I told you about my wife and all she has done for our family. Now, I want to expand that and tell you about our village that helps us! It truly does take a village to get all the things done that together we have been able to get Will to do. Many times we get a lot of the credit, but in all reality we have just been the fortunate ones to facilitate it all. As we go through all the help we have been given, in no means can I list every person who has played a part in the success that our family has

attained. As this is being written, there are countless others who are playing just as vital a roll as those you will read about in the following pages. They are listed in no particular order of importance because they would all be listed #1. We need them ALL!

Therapists have played a very key role in our success. One of the main therapists who has been through the valleys as well as the mountain tops with us is Lynn, Will's longtime occupational therapist. She has put her foot in Will's back so to speak and mine, too, but always been there to pick him up when the task or the demands were too great for him to handle. She has had to convince me on several occasions that this was what was best for Will especially before I really bought into what all we were trying to do for him. She has pushed him into a lot of things that I never dreamed he would be able to do nor would have even thought of doing with him. One instance is Acts Jr. "Acts" is a theater program put on by Community Connections, a local nonprofit. It is designed for special needs kids and some of their typically developing peers to put on a theater production. They do it each spring and fall during the school semester and then have a production at the end of the semester. If you will remember I said that he was diagnosed as nonverbal? Well, he has had a speaking part in the last several productions, some of which he has said his line or words and some of which he hasn't. Regardless, he has had speaking parts! I would have never even thought he would have participated much less had a part like that. Lynn did, and she believed he could do it. He certainly has, and he looks forward all summer long for the fall to start and all winter getting ready for the spring to start.

The next therapist is Diana, Will's speech therapist. Yes. I said speech therapist! The one constant in Will's therapy life is speech. The problem is he has had many speech therapists, and if you know anything about therapy that is not a good thing. Diana has been with us for several years now and is making tremendous strides with his speech. For example, she has given him a standard speech evaluation for the past several years and has only been able to do the first of three parts of it because of his lack of speech. But the last time she did an evaluation, she was able to do all three parts of this evaluation for the very first time because of the strides he has made with his language capabilities. They told me he would never speak... need I say more?

Will has great therapists at school, too, that see him on a weekly basis. Karen and Ashley are his OT and Speech therapists at school and have worked with him for a couple of years. They have seen tremendous strides along our road that we are paving every day. Karen has taught Will how to tie his shoes! Apparently he already knew how and no one realized it. He is pretty smart. Ashley has seen a lot of strides in Will's speech over the past few years as well. He is very compartmentalized and often times won't do the same things for different people in different places. Therefore, a lot of the things they have been able to accomplish we have not yet seen outside of school, and some of what we have done, they have not been able to see at school.

It takes a village to do this, and the therapists in our lives have made a major impact upon our growth. They have fought for him, with him, and about him. We could not do what we do without them, nor are we going to try. They have made a huge impact in all of our lives.

Family also makes a huge impact on our lives as they would in any situation. We have a lot of family who are always ready to lend a hand and help with anything they can.

The first I want to mention is my mother in law, Brenda. She and my father-in-law were foster parents and therapeutic foster parents for over twenty years. They have encountered all types of things when it comes to children and special needs. They have brought countless children into their home over the years and tried to give each and every one of them the same care and consideration that they did their two biological children. My wife is the oldest of the seven children. She has one biological sister and five adopted brother and sisters. Brenda has been the mother to a number of children over the years, whether it was a child they brought into their home or to the ones they come in contact with every day. There have been countless times over the past several years that she has been the voice of reason, consultation, or the one who said, "This is what you need to do." She, like all the rest of us, has not always had the "right" answer but the answers she has provided have given us countless ideas and remedies for some of the issues we have faced. She has shown me what it truly means to love unconditionally. No one said it was always the easy thing to do, but she has certainly been a model of that.

Next, my parents Mickie and Judy. I know without a doubt this has not been an easy road for either of them. It is one thing to walk through something yourself, but another to be a part of something with your son and grandson. MY mom was the one, who when Will was first diagnosed, told me she had no idea what we needed to do or what we were going to do, but we would figure it out with God's help. In all reality, besides giving you the book that will tell you exactly how and what to do in every situation, what more could you ask for? They have been the rock behind the scenes for all of my life. They will be the first to admit they have made mistakes just like the rest of us, but I will tell you that I could not or would not be here today if it were not for them.

If any of you have ever been through a "rough spot" in your life, you will understand why these next three people are another reason I am still here today making a difference in this world. I have three friends that I have had for years that when the tough got going, every friend I thought I had left me but these three. Mark, Kevin, and Chad, each in their own unique way, are the reasons I am here. There were many times I wanted to pack it in and leave and they would not hear of it, and they would come do whatever it was they had to do to smooth the edges. Some of those things we could talk about. (And some are better left where they are!) True friends are there when no one else is, and they see the things that no one else wants to see. The Word says that "the steps of a righteous man are ordered by God", and I believe that to be true. I have no doubt that for such a time as this I have been truly blessed with some amazing friends that would not let me quit. They will tell you that they need or deserve no credit whatsoever, but I tell a different story. I needed them and they showed up!

Jim and Norma, otherwise known as Grandpa and Mimi, are Will's grandparents, my ex-wife's parents. They have been a huge factor in his success over the years. Will goes to their house every other weekend and some extended stays during the summer. Grandpa and Will like to go out to the farm and ride the tractor and work the cattle on the weekends. Will loves to be outside, so he and Grandpa get along just fine! Mimi loves to whip Will up some great food and Will loves to eat it! They have been a huge influence in his life and have helped a great deal with Will learning to transition from place to place, which is a difficult task for him.

Will has two sisters that have had and will continue to have a huge impact upon his life. He has an older sister, Emma, and a younger one, Anna Katherine, we call Kate. Obviously, Emma has been here for his entire life and has been a fantastic big sister. She has played with and tried to get him to do a variety of things over the years. Emma wants to be a doctor one day and I believe she will make a great doctor to some really deserving patients one day! Kate, his younger sister, has assumed all of those rolls at this point because they have a pretty unique bond now. They still like a lot of the same stuff, and she is so very patient with him. She often tells us that she wants to be a Special Ed teacher one day, and I believe she has the gift for what that takes. They both love their brother beyond measure and you do not dare mess with him or you will have two sisters on you quickly.

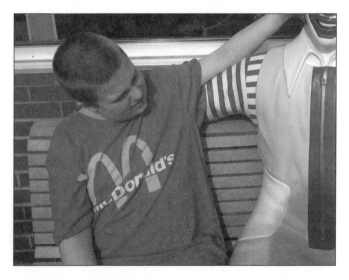

Then there are a lot of people and entities that have certainly been the help that we all needed at different times throughout our years. They are definitely part of the village that has helped us get to this point. Most of them are still very important parts of our daily lives even though we may not "see" them often. We always know that they are there and praying with us.

The first person I want to mention is Pastor Randy at The Church Alive in Conway, AR. Pastor Randy has had a tremendous influence in all of our lives over the years that we have lived in the area. He has believed with us from the first moment we met him years ago that the potential God has in Will is much greater than what the eye can see or the mind can conceive. He has been a constant prayer warrior for us, as well as numerous other people at The Church Alive. I will never forget as long as I live the September morning in 2012 that Will said, "Jesus" in the microphone down front. It was a turning point in all our lives for sure!

Another very important place we have been a part of for a long time is Pediatrics Plus. This is the therapy center in Conway, Arkansas, where Will has had Occupational, Speech and Physical Therapies since he has lived with us for over seven years. We have had several therapists over the years that have helped us along the way. They are too many to mention, but we owe all of them a debt of gratitude for their sacrifice and help!!

There is another group of individuals who deserves more credit than probably any other group. That group is our caretakers. Babysitters is not very accurate. We are definitely giving some real world education to some amazing college kids that are going to make some great parents and educators one day! Walking through hot coals for some of them would be less difficult than some of the roads they have had to walk with us. Bobby, Taylor, Eileen, Ron, Zach, Molly, Aaron, Meghan, Kori, Ellie, and Judah have played amazing roles in our lives and our ability to help Will and do what we do! Thank you all!

Last, but certainly not least, is school. For a lot of families with kids with special needs, public school is a very scary and intimidating place. To ever say that it hasn't been for us to some degree would not be totally accurate. However, we have been blessed with some great staff members at school that we have had the privilege to work with over the years. It takes cooperation from both sides to make this work. We all have to be willing to do what is in the best interest of the child for it to work, and then both be willing to make the sacrifices necessary.

There have been many people involved over the years but the top of the list goes to Mrs. Courtney. She was the self-contained teacher throughout most of Will's elementary years. She definitely endured a lot of things and gave of herself unselfishly for the betterment of a lot of children in her class and not just mine. She helped Will go to lunch with the rest of the class, share the swing, keep his clothes on, sit and do work at the table, wash and dry clothes, wash his hands and many other things some of which I was told he would never do. The one thing that stands out in my mind is the notes we would get home sometimes daily for a while that would say, "Today wasn't a great day, but tomorrow will be better." She never wavered, that we could see, and always tried to be positive. She will never truly understand what an impact that had in order for all of us to stay the course.

The next person is Mr. Ron. Ron was the first special education supervisor that I ever had the privilege of working with at school. He was a very kind and understanding administrator to me and always took time to help me understand a lot of the inner workings of the special education world. Even after Ron had moved on from our school district, he has been a very important person in my life to help me manage this road we are trying to pave for my son. Ron has had an impact on our lives both professionally and personally over all these years. I anticipate this will continue for many, many, years to come.

There have been several para professionals over the years that have played an extremely vital role in our lives. Lindsey, Mary, Bailey, Stacey, Jenny, Donna, Andi, Judy, and Cristie, as well as many others! These ladies have had a great deal to do with our success in the past and in the future. They are the backbone of what we have tried to accomplish over the years of school. We love each of them and appreciate all they have been through with Will and have done for him.

There are many therapists, teachers, and administrators who have been a vital part as well. Mr. Scott, Ms. Sonya, Mrs. Kim, Mrs. Lisa, Mrs. Denise, Mrs. Sue, Mrs. Amy, Mrs. Shannon, Mrs. Kathy and the many others that there is no way I could mention them all. Thank you is not enough to say or no way could I adequately thank each of them properly. One day when Will can speak, and walks across that stage to get his diploma, I pray he is able to tell each of you 'thank you' himself!

As you can see, our village is a huge part of what and who we are. It is also a very important part of where we have the ability to go in the future. There are many of our friends and family who are here for us and constantly pray with us for Will. Life sometimes throws curve balls. I was never good at hitting a curve ball. However, I have definitely been blessed with people in our lives who not only can hit the curves we get thrown, but they do so with a smile. I love you all and I appreciate your willingness not only to walk the mile with us but you are going the extra miles that we are having to walk. Our lives will never be the same!

"The smartest man is not the one who knows the most or thinks he knows the most. It's the one who surrounds himself with people that are smarter than he is!" Kris Shinn

CH6 THE OTHER SIDE

I am very blessed to have an older brother in my life. He has always been someone I could talk to about things, bounce ideas off of from time to time, and get instruction from if he thought I needed it. Siblings are definitely a gift from God for so many reasons. I have two daughters that are on either side of my son, so he is blessed with an older and younger sister. I want them to know how much I appreciate them and how blessed we are to have them. They each in their own way are very special, and I know that God chose them, as well as the rest of us, to be a part of this life. They have that child-like faith that we are supposed to have, and I look up to them in a lot of ways.

Siblings in a special needs family have a tremendous responsibility placed on their lives. They are sometimes a caretaker, at other times a parent, and

best of all a friend. I want to tell them what I want them to know for their lives ahead and some perspective from where they have been as well.

1: Respect...... is what I have for each of you. It takes special people to live in a family with special needs individuals. You have my utmost respect for how you treat your brother and how you help others to do the same. It cannot always be easy nor fun to do what you have to do sometimes, but I respect you for loving your brother the way you do.

2: Honor......for the adults you are becoming. Both of you are very special in your own way. Time will tell what you are to become. Who you are is so much more than I could have ever dreamed who you would be. The way you are makes it such an honor for me to be your dad.

3: Love.....cannot begin to tell how strong my feelings are for you. You stick through stuff that most of us would never dream about doing for ourselves, not to mention for our own sibling. I love you girls more so than I can say or show some days. I hope you always know that and will love your families the same!

4: Admiration......for the way you conduct yourselves in regards to everything we walk through with your brother. Through the meltdowns in the store or the water park, to the times we have all shined together in shows. I admire how you treat him as you would someone you care dearly for and love.

5: Laughter.....that you provide in the mist of the storms of life sometimes that we all face together. Your smiles can light up the room even in the darkest of times. Your humor can make the day seem just a little bit better. Please keep that smile, sense of humor, and the attitude that keeps smiles on those around you.

6: Attitude......is very contagious. The way you carry yourselves and the way you show others how your brother should be treated is something I am very proud of in all cases. It is very difficult sometimes to have the right attitude walking this road, but you seem to do a wonderful job. Always be positive and keep the best attitude.

7: Faith........is encouraging, how you use it and believe. I have often asked God to give me the amount of faith that you each have to know that God is in control. Your faith is made evident in what you say and do in this world. Let your light shine for all to see!

8: Hope.....in what lies ahead for each of you. The future is bright for each of you, and as we walk this road out together you will have a bright future ahead. I am amazed at the hope I see in your eyes and your actions. Spread that hope that you see and have among those that you encounter. You are the generation that will make the difference.

9: Acceptance.... of what lies behind and what will be in the road ahead. You will be able to teach others that come along how they should treat others and what they should do. Your acceptance of this road you have been asked to walk along with us reveals the true nature of God that each of you possess.

10: Example.....of what a life worth living looks like. You are a true picture of what and how we were intended to be towards one another in this life. You get up and put one foot in front of the other each and every day. Realizing that none of it is fair, you keep pressing forward helping your siblings who need it the most!

11: The next Generation.........is what you are a part of that we are raising in this world that will be able to help everyone learn what to do. You accept things just the way they are, but see the best in your brother. You will be great employees and members of society that everyone will want to have around them. Please, always keep your hearts and minds focused on God and He will direct your paths.

There is so much that needs to be said in regards to the hearts of the siblings that are on the road the rest of us are on in regards to special needs families. Sometimes they are forgotten in the everyday dealings that we all seem to get caught up in doing for the kids. They are important and they should be treated as such. If we want to raise the generation that we all wish we had grown up in, we must learn to accept those kids that we are all now raising!

Time will tell how good of a job we do. I for one hope that people already see the difference my kids are making in their worlds not only to make it better for them, but for their siblings with special needs. I salute all you who have siblings with special needs who have fought the fight and kept the faith! They may never be able to tell you thanks in this world, but one day they will!

CH7 SCHOOL

"For I know the thoughts I think toward you..."- Jeremiah 29:11.

The road was made before each of us was ever born into this world. The plan for my life was set and made. Please do not think for one minute that I have not been angry, mad or upset as I have traveled this road I am on. This is not the road I had envisioned for my life, nor any of my family. However, my faith is not in my own abilities or strengths, but in God.

Often one of the most difficult places that our kids have to navigate is school. I am not sure how it was when you grew up, but I remember back when I was growing up that all of the special education classrooms where on the other end of the school from the regular education classrooms. We never really saw any of those kids except maybe going back and forth to lunch or coming out for recess when we were coming back inside. My mother was a teacher in the school districts I grew up in and recalled only on several occasions that any of the special education kids were in our classes or in her classroom. Self-contained, IEP, Resource, 504...are just some of the terms that have entered my vocabulary in the last several years. Oh, how times have changed and should change.

Some of you may be thinking at this point you cannot wait to hear what I have to say about school and how bad it is for our kids. Well, I hate to disappoint you. Now, to say we have not had our share of turmoil would not be totally accurate. I challenge each of you to think back and remember if you have had any challenges in your life? If you can't think of any; ask someone who knows you, and I assure you they will have at least one. I want to challenge you to listen to what I am about to tell you and challenge you with in the next several pages. It will serve you and your children well, as well as pave the way for the other parents and children.

I remember the day in early October in 2007 when we went to pick up Will to come live with us. There was great anticipation and some anxiety as we drove towards the pickup location to get him. My eyes filled with some tears realizing that he was actually coming to live with Brandi and me. All those thoughts of him leaving with his sisters and mother several years before came flooding back into my memory as we got closer.

We drove up and they were there waiting for us. Will sat quietly in the car as we talked and exchanged a lot of his things. He really had no idea what was about to happen and how all our lives were about to change......for the better! At that time, he was having a lot of trouble staying in school and they really had no idea what to do with him or what to do for him. Little did I realize that I didn't either. Fortunately for all of us, Brandi did.

We put him in our car and began to drive back home. He did really well in the car, and we made the trip just fine. He already had his own room at our house with all of his stuff in it. We put away his things that came with him, and he settled in really well. He already knew all these surrounding so it wasn't quite as much of a transition as it could have been.

What we encountered the following days ahead I can assure you I was nowhere close to being ready for. We had already contacted the school the day before we picked him up preparing them that he was coming. We also had contacted the place where he would get a lot of his therapies and prepared them for his arrival.

As we took him to school the first day, he was only able to stay an hour. It took us several months in order to get him to stay the whole day. I am not really sure how any of us survived. Only by the grace of God did we make it through that period of time.

At the end of that semester we decided to change elementary schools in the town we live in. There are three of them now, each are K-5. The teacher at the other school that we had wanted Will to attend was much more knowledgeable and willing to work with us and Will. We had to petition the administration to move schools. Our first petition was denied; I had to go meet with the Superintendent. I met with him and we were able to get that done for Will, and oh, what a difference it has made for him! For several weeks at the end of the semester, we had them take Will over to the new school and we picked him up from there so that he would get accustomed to that ending of his day.

Once summer had begun, we had to drive him to school every day for about three weeks to show him that no one was there. He loves routine, and each of us had a great deal to learn. After those three weeks, we had a really long summer because of our lack of routine and not much going on in his world. There were many trips to Magic Springs and the Travelers games that summer with all the kids. Finding things to be able to do that keep everyone entertained is not always an easy task. We have done many things and tried many places before we found things that work! Do not fret because you are not alone in that arena!

When school began in the fall, the first several weeks were pretty rough with phone call, emails, texts, and numerous trips to the school. I am sure right now that many of you are also walking this road and can understand exactly what I have said. You are not alone! Through many trials and errors, we were able to get some consistency going, and the bumps were smoothing out a bit.

Then came the time when Will wanted to take his clothes off every day. Yes, he wanted to go naked at school. Now as you can imagine and even may be able to empathize with, this was not acceptable. Will had figured out that if he would take his clothes off at school they would make him go to the bathroom, and he would get out of doing his work. Smart! (He is his daddy's son!) We finally broke him of this because Brandi went up to the school and sat in the bathroom all day with him until 4:45. He finally did his work realizing everyone was leaving. She had to return to the school the following day, and they sat in the bathroom for about an hour until he finally realized she could and would outlast him. We have not had much trouble with that since! We just had to outsmart and outlast him. At that time, it was not nearly as unacceptable for him at age seven as it would be now at age thirteen or even later in life at twenty-one. We all have to do what we need to do now in order to get them ready to walk out into the world one day.

We have had many ups and downs through our school days. We fight battles all the time, but as time has gone on we all realized that we are on the same team and that is for the benefit of my son. You have to realize that the school is not the enemy, but they also have to realize that our families are different, and we have lives that are in no way ordinary. It has to work both ways. You have to realize that they aren't there just for the benefit of your child nor mine. They are there to help all kids. There are a lot of kids there and each deserves the opportunities to succeed. Time will only tell how this will work out for us all. There is nothing wrong with the fight as long as it is for the benefit of the kids. They deserve our best. We need to give them our best everyday all day long and sometimes all night long!

We have to always remember that the victory is worth the battle. Victory may be light years away in our mind, but it is worth every tear drop and sweat drop shed over the years. No one can understand a special needs family like another one. I believe in my heart that most schools want to do what is in the best interest of the child. Obviously, there are exceptions to that rule as we all know. However, like most of the families, most of the school personnel don't have all the answers either. They are sometimes just as puzzled as we are and sometimes even more! We have to work as a team, both sides! Our kids are worth it! Every child is worth it. I challenge you wherever you may be standing in this constant battle to try and put your feet in the others' shoes who are trying, too. Our perspective a lot of times is worse than the actual facts. The goal at school is to help each child become a functional member of society by the time he graduates. We MUST work as a team. There are no excuses for not, and the child will be the real loser in the end

if we do not. The other side is not the enemy, whichever side you are standing on. You will be well served remembering that fact. Do not be the enemy!

CH8 ALL ABOUT PERSPECTIVE

Down this road there have been many miles that I have had to travel that I never knew even existed. Lessons there are that I have learned that I never even knew I would need to learn nor knew were available to learn. The best part about all that is there are many more that are ahead of me, and I am looking forward to learning them well as to help more and more kids out there. It is all about perspective. My perspective will help dictate what it looks like from here, not whether or not we will travel the roads. Here are a few examples.........

One day I was at work and my phone rang just like many other times. I looked at the phone, and it was my wife Brandi calling me. I answered the phone and she told me that I needed to come home that she needed some help. Without many more questions, I left and went home. I have learned over time that if she calls me and asks me to come home that I just need to head that way. Questions just lengthen the time that I can leave and get there and get control over the situation. As I arrived at home, I had no real idea what I was going to walk into when I came in. This was not the first time I had this feeling, and I am real sure it will not be the last as well. Anyway, I walked in and she and the girls were in the kitchen. Not really what I had envisioned walking into after the phone call I had gotten. She looked at me and asked me to go see Will in his room. I have never liked this sort of greeting because it has always seemed to be detrimental to Will and me in the past. As I walked into Will's room, he was sitting on his bed watching TV. I am sure the look on my face was worth an untold amount of money because he was...... blue! I was almost speechless as I tried to ask him questions as to what and how this happened. Obviously, he was pretty proud of himself and showed me what all he had done to himself. He was pretty thorough to say the least.

After the show and tell I got from Will, I walked back into the living room and began to laugh out loud at this 'blue boy" that I had just witnessed. I began to ask questions of all three of my girls as to what and how this had happened. Apparently, while they were in the room trying on clothes, Will was going back and forth. He acquired a Sharpie somehow, a single blue regular size Sharpie, and proceeded to color himself blue. Not light blue, but blue! He had done an excellent job coloring himself in a very limited amount of time. We watch him like a hawk, and he had managed in that very short time to do a great job.

Later in the evening, we were preparing to go out to eat like we do a lot it seems. At that time, he was around seven years old which means his younger sister was around five. As we began to get everyone ready to go, Kate comes into our bedroom and begins to ask us if Will was going to eat with us. My wife explained to her that he was going and we couldn't just leave him at home. She said, "But he is blue. Don't you think people are going to look at him and us funny?" As I tried to keep from falling out in the floor laughing, my wife told her, "Do you not think that people already looked at us and him that way?" She said, "Well, yeah, but not because he is blue but because he has autism!" See it was ok to her that people looked at us like we were strange because he had autism but not because he was blue. There is a lesson for all of us in the way she views that.

We tried everything known to man that anyone told us to try to get the blue off him but to no avail. It took about six weeks for all the blue to finally fade. The imprint of that blue boy will live with all of us forever though. We all loved that little blue boy!

The next story I want to share is an ongoing story. Several years ago, we were able to get Will an iPad for his birthday. It was a collaboration between a lot of people for us to be able to get that for him. We are forever grateful. The first couple of times we tried to get him to use the iPad he wasn't really interested. As time went by, he became more and more interested. We then noticed that he was getting on YouTube and watching videos and saving them. We had not set up an account for him to be able to do that. I was able to watch over his shoulder one day and noticed he was logging on to an account. The only place that he had access to that would have been at school. Well, we went and spoke to his teacher about it, and she assured us that she had not set him up an account or given him access to hers. Then she told us she had noticed a lot of kid videos showing up on her saved account. I asked her to change her password and take the videos off, and we would monitor the situation closer to see if we could see what he was doing. After about a week, she noticed those same videos showing up again. I had also noticed he was typing in an account and password. The more I dug into it the more I began to realize it was hers. He had been able to recognize the clicks off the Smart Board at school and was able to input them into his iPad, getting into her account all from the sounds. I was floored, she was floored, and we knew at that point we had to step up our game!

She changed her password to a more complex one and as of today he still hasn't figured it out. I did set him up an account under my name so he can now save them himself and not hack his teachers account. It was kind of funny to us all at the time and we all learned a valuable lesson. Since then he has watched a variety of videos on YouTube. To date, we have counted up to at least seventeen different languages that he has watched videos in…that we know of. Some of them are pretty interesting to say the least. If you have never heard Scooby Doo in French you are missing out! Do I think he understand all those languages? I am unsure of to what extent he understands any of them. I do think he does to some degree. He is amazing in so many areas and this is one we continue to facilitate for now and will continue into the future.

We have to make many daily decisions that most parents never even consider. One of which is where we can go out to eat. Will, just like many kids with special needs, has tunnel vision. They are only concerned with their world unless they are required to think about others. So, when we go out somewhere for dinner, there are a lot of considerations that have to especially be made. Noise level is a big consideration. He cannot handle some of the loud noises, especially the high pitched ones. If we know places like this we avoid them if at all possible with him. Also, we go places that have booths. Once he gets done eating, he is ready to go no matter if everyone else is or not! With Will being lactose intolerant, we do not go to many Mexican restaurants with him because he won't understand that he cannot have the cheese dip they serve. Just as you wouldn't go to an Italian place if you had someone in your party that was allergic to gluten!

We have exercise balls in our house that not only does Will like to sit on, but our two girls do as well! Will can get on all fours on top of his exercise ball and balance himself. It is pretty amazing to watch him do this. We didn't teach him to do that, but I am sure he has done it in OT and maybe has seen one of his sisters do it.

It is all about perspective you see. You can look at the disability, or you can choose to look at the "abilities". He has so many more abilities than he has disabilities as we see it. The issue is figuring out how to get those out of him in a way that he can utilize for his future. It is truly all about perspective. It is his perspective that is the challenge to see and to help him to grow into a productive member of society. It is his life, not mine nor yours. I challenge you to examine your perspectives and thoughts. I challenge you to think outside the box and see what can happen. Will it be easy....no! Will it be worth it.....no question!

CH9 HOW/WHY WE DO IT

I often have people ask me, "Kris, how do you do it?" I have often also had people ask me, "Kris, why do you do it?" To me, these are pretty simple questions to answer. But, the more I think about it the more I find reasons that most probably have never even been thought about or have any concept about. The phrase, you never really know what you can or will do unless you are faced with that situation, has really never been more true in my life than over the past eleven plus years. Here are a few reasons of how and why!

The main reason of how Brandi and I do it is pretty simple and some will like it and some will not. That's totally in your court, but I assure you He is the reason! God in His infinite wisdom saw fit to have me of all dads to be able to raise my son and daughters. He knew before the foundations of the world that He needed me to be the dad that would go the extra mile and beyond for Will. His purpose is not always clear, but His love never fails. He has a plan, and I am just so thankful to be just a small part of it. I had a conversation with my brother years ago about the fact that I wanted him to be praying with me for Will's healing. I know it will happen one day, however, it may not be on this earth but when we cross over into Heaven. My brother called me one day sometime later to discuss it with me. As we began our conversation he asked me what I thought is the greatest problem facing the world? Obviously that was a loaded question because how can you boil that down to one? He then began to explain to me that he believes it is pride. Pride is a very interesting problem because in can encompass a lot of other things, and thus he said he believed that it is the biggest issue we have. He then asked me an interesting question. He said, "Does Will have any pride?" I sat and began to think about that and the answer was, "No, none at all". You see, he doesn't care if you drive the right car or if you live on the right side or wrong side of the tracks. He could not care less how much money you have or don't have (unless you are buying at McDonalds), nor does he care who you are or are supposed to be, and he doesn't care what nationality or color your skin is either! All he really wants to know is do you care? As we began to talk further we then realized that it is probably us who needs prayer not Will. Obviously I would prefer that he be able to function in this world that was not made for him, but in true reality it was not made for me either because I am just passing through. So it is by the grace of God. That answer's how!!

The other question I get asked a lot is, "Why do you do it?" My question is then "Why would I not do it?" We do it because he is our son. He is worth whatever it is that we need to do to help him in any way possible. If that means getting less sleep, missing out on ballgames, not going out to eat, missing some live church services, sitting in only certain seats at events, not going to some things because it might upset him, repeating the same thing over and over for years but to finally one day see it happen, so be it! Is it the life that I had dreamed of years ago? To be honest, no it is not. Would I have it any other way at this point? Not a chance! Will is THE best teacher I have ever had in my life, and I continue to learn so much from him each and every day. Is it easy? Not at all, but it is so worth it! Another reason we do it is because the world looks at individuals like my son as 'the least of these'. It is a sad day when that happens because the Word says, "As you have done unto the least of these, you have done unto Me." God knew their abilities before they were ever born. He didn't do this to them, but He does make a way where there seems to be no way. He does say that all things are possible to those who believe. I will never stop believing, and I will never stop fighting this battle. Never give up or give in because there is no victory without a battle!

One of the biggest reason why we do it is for the others. That road we are paving, they will get to drive on. At this point, I can think of no better thing in this world that I would rather be doing than to be in business with my wife at Above All Else, Inc. We have an Autism and Behavioral Consulting Business based in Central Arkansas. Brandi has been teaching professional development since the year 2000, and I joined her in the fall of 2012 after being in sales for over twenty years. This is the most rewarding work I have ever done. I have often been quoted as saying, "We are real people, offering real solutions, in a real world, to help real people with problems." If we help the individuals with special needs, then it is a win-win situation for all concerned! We are on the forefront of the diagnosis train that is now at full steam ahead. We are battling some of the things that some of those who come behind us will get to enjoy and not have to fight. Is it worth it for those families? Absolutely! Do we draw strength from them as well? Yes we sure do! It is all about the kids and giving them all the opportunities that we can possibly give them in order for them to succeed!

We also do it because we have a very unique perspective that we can offer the schools and the families. My wife, as you read in a previous chapter, was a special education teacher for many years. Then we are also parents of a child with special needs, so we can offer insight to both sides of the aisle so to speak. We can understand who, what, when, where, how and sometimes why the school views things the way they do as well as the families or parents. It has been a real eye opener for me as to how some of both sides never really communicate to try and do what is best for the individual. TOO many times we get caught up in what we think we know or what we think someone said and do not really get together and discuss things. Our kids are worth the effort whatever it takes for us to communicate with each other. We are not always going to see eye to eye on everything. But, if we will come to the table with open hearts and minds and a regard for what is best for the individual, we may just be amazed at what the children are capable of in the long run.

With getting the privilege to be in so many settings and to see so many ways to do things, it has enabled us to provide a better setting for Will in many ways. I liken it to the hamster on the wheel. Most see that he is just going in circles, but maybe if we looked closer, could he possibly be doing it a better way every time? The privilege of being in so many homes and schools has given us the ability to not only help our own son even more, but it has broadened our scope on how we can help other individuals, families and schools. It is a win-win situation all the way around. There has been nothing more rewarding for me than to see success and hope in people's eyes. When you can help give them hope, you change their lives.

The "hows" and the "whys" have changed over the years and I am really confident that they will continue to change in the future. The fact still remains at the end of the day it is all about helping people. People with real issues trying to navigate a real world in which most have no idea which direction to turn. At the very beginning of this chapter I explained how we do it and how I do it. I know no other way nor do I need to. God has my back and He always will. There are a lot of occasions that I need a reminder, and it is amazing how He does that for me most of the time through Will. I believe he is God's Will (not just my Will), and I have a great responsibility to raise him in a way that will be pleasing to Him. Do I fail? Daily. But I have decided to pick myself up, dust myself off, and go again! All my kids deserve that and those are not just the ones that live with me. The kids, families, and school personnel who depend on us to help them are worth the effort each and every day. We definitely do not have all the answers; no one does. But we do depend on the One who does! Though none go with me...... STILL, I will follow!

CH10 CHALLENGES

For the most part, thus far, I have described a lot of things, people and places in this journey. I want to talk in this chapter about the many challenges we face on a day to day, week to week basis that may surprise you, or you may even understand. Most families will never let you know some of these things, and those of you who are reading this who live this life will be relieved to know you are not the only ones! Some of these things may be humorous to you, and some may make you cry, some may make you think a little differently about us, and some may give you the urge to help someone next time. I challenge you to think about some of these things the next time you see something you do not understand!

One of the main challenges that we encounter is the communication problems. If you remember back in the first chapter the doctors told me that Will would never speak. They also told me he would have to possibly be in an institution by the time he was twelve. We live in a verbal world, and if you are non-verbal, you are going to have a very difficult time surviving. You are also going to communicate the only way you know how and most of the time that is phys-

ically. We all know that babies cry for numerous reasons, and if you think about it that is the only way they have to communicate. We use the skills we have until we gain new skills that are better, for the most part. As most kids grow and learn to talk they can explain why, but we as parents have to guess. When you are a non-verbal child, for the most part, you tend to do those things which get you what you want. You would point, just take what you want, you might hit someone if they made you mad, or you might push them out of your way. Many devices that have been in use for a while now can assist in helping these individuals communicate in the world they are living in. As time has gone by, the technology has increased so much that now we have some really nice portable devices that everyone carries that can be used as well. The older the individuals get, the more damage can be done if we do not give them ways to communicate.

As Will has gotten older, his vocabulary has increased greatly, and his physical attempts to get what he wants have decreased. This is a very good thing because the doctor tells me he may grow to be 6'4" and over 300 lbs. I don't know about you, but that big fella will be a handful at that point! He is very versed on his iPad, and we hope that it will continue to help facilitate his communication in the future. I am not sure how well he may be able to communicate in complete sentences; but I do know he is talking some and can answer questions. Communication is a very vital challenge.

Another challenge is keeping his clothes on. I know that most of you who have special needs children just either got a smile on your face or started crying depending upon where you are in this stage! Most parents have had kids that went through a stage of wanting to take their clothes off at the most inappropriate times and places. Well, when you are four or five years old, it is much different than when you are a teenager! Remember that we had some times when Will was in elementary school that he took off his clothes to get out of doing his work. You can't let a naked kid sit in any class to do his work. No one really wants to sit in the bathroom with a naked kid all day either trying to get their clothes on, much less do some work. Well, my wife spent one whole day in the bathroom at school with Will until he realized everyone was going home because the lights went off. All of a sudden he did his work and put his clothes on. He tried it the next day and this time it only took less than an hour and he pretty much stopped doing that at school. Now, he has had his moments at school and other places over the years still, but not to the degree it was in the past.

Another challenge that we have faced is constant change. In most of our kid's world change or transition is a nightmare most days...at best. Will does not like change and for a long time we were unsure of what all exactly he could understand. Just because he cannot have a conversation with you like others doesn't mean he cannot understand. In fact, he probably understands a lot more things than most of us do! New clothes, new bedrooms, new TV, new schools, new classes, new teachers, new places to eat, new jobs for parents, new schedules, new help at home...all of which can be a total and complete nightmare. But, they can also be great teaching times and moments because that is the way the world works at present. Change is inevitable in everyone's life and the better we are able to handle it, the better survival skills become. I say a lot of times in some of the classes I teach that there is a reason we do not put fourth graders in Geometry. For the majority, they could not handle it and would have no clue how to work any problems even with the best teacher ever! They aren't ready for that and thus the same for a lot of our kids. They are not ready to handle a ton of change. However, it is going to happen at some point, and we as families have to do everything we possibly can to get them ready for that change. It is in no way an easy thing to do nor think about, but it is reality. If we ever want them to walk out the door one day and be functional, it is what we have to do for them!

A very significant challenge is the puberty issues. Oh yes, we all go through that regardless of disability or ability. Your body does change regardless and those challenges can be extremely tough. These changes have to be addressed by someone and cannot be ignored. Families most often seem to have the hardest time with this, and sometimes it never crosses their minds until they are right in the middle of it. It is obviously hard on the school to deal with because most have never had to go that extra mile or three to help curb some of those urges and actions. It really has to be a concentrated effort on all sides to come up with a great plan to help the individuals deal with the changes that they are experiencing.

Another challenge is acceptance. We do now have Autism Awareness Month every April, and at this point if you are not "aware" of it, you might live in a cave. We need more acceptance than anything. I do not know of a single individual or family who asked to have autism. It is not known to be a deadly disease, but it has some tremendous challenges that go with it. The individuals are going to make sounds, have meltdowns, and not understand everything thing socially that some of the rest of us do. In fact, there are a lot of people in this world who do not get some things that we all think everyone should. Will doesn't understand that everyone's drink doesn't belong to him, he has to be taught. He doesn't understand that you cannot walk down the middle of the street, he has to be taught. Many of us had to learn the hard way that the stove was actually hot and get burned. That is a really difficult thing when your child doesn't sense fear. We need to accept them for who they are and try and help them learn. Most families will never ask for your help, but I assure you they need it. They just want to be accepted just like everyone else and not be excluded. Most parents or family members feel isolated anyway, so I challenge you to go out of your way to make them feel accepted. Be warned though, they may not take you up on an offer because they do not want to be a burden on anyone. Offer anyway!

The next challenge is eating and meal time. Many of our kids have different allergies and texture issues with food. Different smells will affect them as well. Most of our kids are not really social beings and therefore would rather eat by themselves. You just have to pick your battles one at a time and tackle different things at different times. No one likes whole-sale changes all the time. Think before you act. As I say that, I am reminding myself as well! We decided a long time ago that we would probably never have family meals like we did when we were growing up. Did we like that? Not really, but you learn to roll and adjust as needed. Pick your battles. Will is what we call a grazer. He will come and eat for a little bit and then go do his own thing. He will be back to get another bite or two at times later. I can hear some of you going, "There is no way I would let my child do that." That is completely fine with me, too. You pick your battles. I will not pick yours, and you will not pick mine. It is pretty simple.

We all have sensory issues I have come to realize. I will not eat Jello for anyone, of any flavor, at any time! I cannot stand for it to be in my mouth. Will loves most of his food almost burnt. He loves the strong taste of things and will not eat anything that might possibly not be cooked thoroughly! He will blow up his hot dogs and cook his pinto beans for almost ten minutes in the microwave. It is a very interesting choice, but that is the way he likes his food. Do I like it that way...no, but he does and will eat it.

I have a lot of sensory issues as well, so I understand some of them. Lights flickering, tags in clothes, sounds that are so high pitched most cannot hear, just to mention a few. There are a lot of individuals that have bones or joints that ache when the weather changes, and a lot of our kids are affected by the pressure change in the atmosphere. We found this out accidentally years ago with Will. I was noticing that every so often he would have bad days at schools for no "apparent" reason. I also starting realizing that on those same days that I was not having the best day either. Then all of a sudden I realized that it was the pending weather change. I started keeping a chart to document it and sure enough about 48 hrs before the weather change we were having issues. I also realized that my allergy and sinus issues might have been inherited to some degree also. When that light bulb finally does come on, it can make you feel very inadequate as a parent but can also provide some relief to know what to do to help your child!

Although this is not a complete list of challenges, these are some of the significant ones that we have faced over the years. I am sure I could list the challenges for years to come and never get to the end of them. Just know you are not alone and the challenges never end, but it is worth helping your child in any way that you possibly can. Use the resources you have available and find new ones. Never quit searching for answers, because in the next chapter we will discuss some of the breakthroughs we have had because The Village we have never would give up!

CH11 BREAKTHROUGHS

This road we are on has had many challenges, but in this chapter I want to focus on the Breakthroughs! Many times all we can see is the forest, but never can see the tree that is there shining brightly bearing all kinds of fruit. I have a really close friend that will remind me often that too many times all we focus on is trying to solve the problems that we face and often do not take the time to enjoy some of the fruits of our labor. We must take stock in that our labor is not in vain. Progress no matter what the size, is still progress. At times there are certain things that we have tried to accomplish that may have taken many repeats on our part or taken years to accomplish. But what if we had never tried? Where would my son or your child be then? I challenge you in whatever field or situation you are in to take stock in the breakthroughs, the victories, and even though to some they may seem small, to some of us they are life changing events!

My wife and I had never been anywhere over two days together away from Will. So last fall we were invited to a conference in Houston, Texas, to be with our good friends Don and Susan at their church. They wanted us to come for five days. We debated and rolled it around and decided that we would try it. We have been very blessed over the years to find some awesome caretakers to help us with Will. He does go to his grandparents every other weekend but usually for just one night. We took him to school on Monday and then flew out later in the day. It was very difficult on us to do this, but we know for his good that we need to do so. Obviously we checked on him numerous times throughout the week, and he did wonderfully. He went to his grandparents on Saturday, and we arrived back home and picked him up on Sunday! We were never really sure how this would work, or even if it would work, but he did great! Sometimes it's the adults who have the biggest issues and not the kids. I know this first hand myself as I struggle with it all it, too. Just because I have a business card or a sign on the side of my car does not mean that I have it all together!

The next breakthrough I want to discuss has to deal with medication. Here is the disclaimer...I am in no way, shape, or form suggesting anyone do anything different than what you are doing or what your doctor says. Several years ago Will was on several meds, and he seemed to start having a lot of issues especially during that summer. I had been talking to a Pastor friend of mine, who at that time lived in North Carolina, Apostle Don. We had been talking for a few minutes, and he asked about Will. I told him we had been having a few issues again with him, and it all seemed revolved around his meds. Apostle Don then said something to me that would change the course of our whole journey. He said, "Kris, I think you need to consider taking Will off those meds." I am sure I had a shocked look on my face not really knowing what to say at that point. I think I just told him that I would have to discuss that with Brandi. He then reiterated it like he knew something. I got off the phone after a few more minutes with him and began to tell Brandi what all he had said. Her reaction I am sure was like most of yours might be right now. He was nuts and there was no way we were doing that! I tentatively agreed even though I am not a huge proponent of medication. It has its uses for sure, but I do think as a society we way over use it instead of figuring out the real problems.

About three weeks later around the first of July, we got out of bed on a Saturday morning, and I asked Brandi if she had given Will his meds. She told me she hadn't and asked me if I had. I said, "No and I am not going to!" Now, at the time, I had no idea where that came from. It was not something I had decided already or really even thought about. She kind of looked at me and told me that was fine because she had to leave for a few days, and if that's what I wanted to do, then I could deal with the problems that would create. We decided not to tell anyone including my daughters so we could see how it would really go. Within three days of our doing that, we saw a different kid. Now, he still takes meds at night to help him sleep, but he has had nothing during the day since then. We have had much better days, and school has been even better. I know He who sent the message; and I am eternally grateful for Apostle Don for delivering His message.

The next breakthrough I want to tell you about, I have already mentioned in another chapter. On Sunday, Sept 9, 2012, at The Church Alive in Conway, AR, was an event I will never ever forget. Several years before I had had a dream or vision of Will in an orange shirt and khaki shorts standing down in front at The Church Alive with the microphone in his hand. That is all I got to see, and I got to hear nothing. Now, remember the doctors told me he would never speak, so to have something like that happen was almost earth shattering for us. I had been telling our pastor that Will had been saying a lot of words and that I had taught him to say Jesus. This was a morning service like most of the others we had at the church, but this morning Will had come in and sat beside me from children's church. He had done this before so it was not a shock or anything to us or anyone else for that matter. Now Will was twizzling his paper as he is accustomed to doing a lot of places when all of a sudden the pastor just stops the music. I mean they are doing worship like crazy this morning, and he just abruptly stops them. He begins to speak, and I knew he was in the process of saying something to me. He then says Kris has been telling me about Will speaking. Everyone in the place knows the diagnosis and believes zero of it like we do. When he says that the place gets loud with applause. He then asks Will if he can say Jesus. Will knows that he is talking to him and gets excited but says nothing. At that point, I grabbed Will by the hand, and we proceed to go up front. Will loves being up front so he was a very willing participant. We get down front, and Pastor Long asks him again if he can say, "Jesus." Will looks at me, and I ask for the microphone. I said, "Will can you say, "Jesus?" Will grabs the microphone and says, "Jesus!" That place went nuts! Literally, for what seemed like forever, it was crazy. Will was loving life at that point as I sat there in tears. You have read where we have come from and know that he was there speaking in the microphone! Whew, it doesn't get much better!

Well, we headed back to our seat for the service. As the pastor wrapped up his message, I looked over at Will and told him how proud I was of him. I noticed something that I hadn't noticed before. That morning I had helped Will get dressed to make sure he matches for his momma! I had picked out a red polo and some khaki shorts. He likes a lot of solid colors! He then went and put the red shirt back and got on orange one. Anyone remember the dream or vision I had? When I realized what had happened and what Will had done, I lost it on the back row. I walked up front with Will after service and reminded the pastor about that vision, and then he looked at Will and we both lost it again. I had gotten to witness the very vision or dream that God had given me. We then created Orange Shirt Ministries as part of Above All Else, Inc. to help churches and special needs families. It was a pretty intense time to say the least, and what a breakthrough!

There have been many more breakthroughs from Will's speech to his learning to manage his emotions and behavior. We have been blessed to have been a part of such an amazing transformation for a young man whom the doctors didn't give much of a chance. However, to limit anyone is to play God, and no one has the right to do that. The sky is the limit, and I cannot wait to see what is next. There will always be a next, and to live this out is more than a good thing. It is truly a miracle in the process. Some may want to disagree with me on that, and by all means they have the right to do so, but as for me, I still believe in what He said. Breakthroughs in my mind are miracles in the process. We are looking forward to seeing and being a part of many, many, more to come!! Hang on because this ride is about to get exciting!

CH12 ...LET. HIM. SOAR!

As parents we seem to want to protect our children a little past when they really need protecting. At times, we do not want to let them touch the stove so that they know it will burn them. As a father of a special needs child, this is even more of an issue because we do not sometimes know what they understand  or what they do not, so we want to protect them as much as we possibly can. This chapter is dedicated to those who made me let him soar and got me out of the box that I wanted to create for him so I could protect him from all of it!

Several years ago, we had an opportunity to send our son to a very well-known camp in central Arkansas. It was a new camp for kids with autism and we had a spot open up at the "last minute" available for our son. If you are very strong in your faith you realize that things don't "just happen"! We quickly filled out the paperwork, and he was in the camp. I was scared to death because I didn't know many, if any, of the people that were running the camp or the counselors at the camp. With a child having autism, who is classified as non-verbal, you are not very quick to trust anyone. If you remember taking your new-born to the nursery the first time at church and how nervous you were, well, we do that on a daily basis. So in all reality, my faith is not in those with whom I leave him with ultimately, but in God above. If my trust was based on humans, I would never let him out of my sight for sure. As the first week went on, he was having a really good time, but we weren't sure how much he was doing. On the last day of the first week my wife went to pick him up after camp, and he ran to the car in the parking lot full of cars. She made him turn around and go back and walk. We had been working on this for months because he has zero sense of danger. As he turned around and walked back to walk back to the car, the counselor who was with him looked at my wife and began to say, "He understood you!" That little man had played those counselors all week into thinking he couldn't understand them and that he needed to be fed all the time! At the time, it was not very funny to me, but as time has gone by it becomes more humorous. It really just shows how smart and cunning he is, and at times you have to outsmart the fox. He has been going to this same camp now for over three years, and they have actually started a new camp for the older kids so that they could continue going. Had it not been for some very smooth talking adults, I might have never let him go. Sometimes even though we live outside of the box, we do not always think outside the box. I want to protect him, but at the same time I have to let him go. It is a very difficult place to be sometimes, but there are reasons for it all. He has made many friends over the last several years and so have the rest of us through his camp. We have seen the struggles of other families in similar situations, and they have watched us in the same light. God makes a way where there seems to be no way at times and in places that we would never dream of or see. God can see it all, and we see but a moment at times. Trust Him, follow Him, and let go sometimes so He can do things that you have never even thought, nor would do, if it wasn't for His guiding hand. He has this, and He has you!

Another interesting place where Will has been able to soar is Special Olympics. If you will remember in Ch. One, I talked a lot about my career and places I had been. When you have been and seen the mountain top in certain areas, it is very difficult to see things from any other perspective. It was a warm spring day in April, and we were at the Area Special Olympics Track and Field Meet. On this particular day, Will was competing in the tennis ball throw and the 50m dash. Now, those of you that know me are chuckling a little right now thinking about the 50m dash. I have always said anything over 25m was a distance event in my book! It was time for the tennis ball throw, and Will did great and won his event! He was proud as he got his medal and he was showing it to me as I was giving him a high five and big hugs! Later on in the day it was time for the 50m dash and you guessed it, he won again! He was so proud of that medal and so were we! We had a great day and all of us, including his two sisters, went and got some lunch at his favorite place, McDonalds. A couple of weeks later, I got a call from my wife that Will had qualified for the State Special Olympics Meet in both of his events. She was so excited and I really think he was when she told him. She was telling me all of what he was going to be able to do and that she was going to take him and spend the night in the dorms with him for the event. She started asking me when I was planning on being there and if the girls would be able to come as well. I didn't respond right away to her, and she could sense some hesitancy in my voice and asked me what was wrong? I changed the subject and started talking about something else. It was a day or two later when we were having to fill out paperwork for her to stay with him when she brought it all up again. This time she didn't let it go and was pinning me down as to what the problem was when we talked about it. I told her that she wouldn't understand, and we would discuss it later. I was hoping she would just forget and not bring it back up. Well, I was wrong. The following week I was in the living room when she came in the house. She began to drill me about it because it was a week before the meet. She asked me, "Ok, what is the issue you are having with this meet?" I began to tell her she wouldn't understand and that she needed to leave me alone about it. She would not give it a rest and kept pressing me on it. Finally, I told her that she would not understand because she had not walked in my shoes. As relentless as she is, I finally broke down and told her. I explained that I had been to the mountain top in my sports career, and it was a long way from there to Special Olympics for me. I think that was the wrong thing to say looking back now. She began to explain to me that I needed to put my big girl panties on and get over it because this was not about me but about our son. That really hit me right between the eyes and I agreed to go.

The girls and I came the following week for the Opening Ceremonies which was the most amazing thing I have ever seen. All those athletes marching in with their respective areas and flags with waves, smiles and tears. After they marched in there was the parade of motorcycles. I have never seen that many motorcycles in one place at one time! Wow is the only way to describe it. The ceremonies wrapped up and the girls and I headed home. The following day we came back and he was competing in the tennis ball throw. As we began to watch him, of all things he was throwing it like a shot put which I know put a smile on my face. After he competed we figured out that he won! He was the State Champ! We all walked over to the awards ceremony tent to watch him get his medal. As the announcer, who was a college friend of mine, announced his name and Will walked up on the awards platform, it hit me like a ton of bricks. It was at that moment that my memory took me back twenty years earlier to that very same spot and same stage where I had won my last conference championship in the shot put and disc. As the tears rolled down my face like they are doing at this moment, I looked up into the clear sky with the sun shining ever so bright and I acknowledged to God above that I finally got it. In a very short time I had come full circle and realized that this was the mountain top that God was bringing me to. I would give up all my plaques, medals, certificates, and rings for that moment to see my son, whom they told me a lot of stuff about, get that medal for winning. The look on his face when they put that medal around his neck was worth more to me that anything this world has ever offered me. I got the biggest hug and smile when he came down. Needless to say, we saw a repeat the following day in the 50m dash as he was once again crowned State Champ! It was a very humbling time in my life, and not that long ago. I have never been more proud of him and the path he is blazing for not only himself but for others to follow!

The last example I want to tell you about is another example from Special Olympics that just happened this year. He didn't qualify in either of his events during the Track and Field Area Games. There would be no State Games this year or so it seemed. The Monday after the Track and Field Area Games we got a call about the possibility of him participating in swimming. I was really hesitant about this because he had never seemed like he would try and swim in a meet. He loves the water a whole lot but to swim in a meet I wasn't real sure about. Once again, I was reminded of what had happened the year before so I told his mom to take him and see what happened. He did really well in the time trials and made the cut for the State Games! The games were again at the same place that we had been the previous year. He was to compete in the 25m assisted and the 25m dash. I wasn't able to be there this time, as I was in another part of the state with my girls at a softball tourney, but I am sure if you listened real well you could have heard me yell when the text came through with a picture of him with his gold medal once again in the 25m assisted! State Champ once again! As the day went on, he did finish third in the 25m dash. So all in all it was a great State Games again. He proved yet again that all he needs is an opportunity!

These are just a couple of great examples of how when given an opportunity that he can soar! Opportunities are what you make them. Too many times we who are in this battle daily cannot see the forest for the trees. We are so consumed with just surviving today that we fail to see what life might be like in the future. (Not your future, but your kids'.) Do not limit them; do not tell them that their dreams and wishes they can be reached! No one has the right to play God nor does anyone have the capacity. Only God has that right. Our kids, all kids deserve the opportunities that we can all try and give them. Walk that mile, run that mile, crawl that mile or two! Whatever it takes to give them all we can and more!

Time will only tell and you make it the best you possibly can! Go for it and 'Let Them Soar'!

CH. 13 EXACTLY WHAT ARE WE DOING

I often get questioned about all of the things that we are doing with Will. They range from people just being inquisitive to some actually being nosey, to those questioning what we are actually doing. Often times now, we do not get a lot of the latter questions. I did want to talk about exactly what we are doing and some of the why's that may come up. We first have to examine the "goal". What is the goal for Will?

If any of you have ever had any dealing with special education then you know what an IEP or a 504 plan is all about. An IEP stands for individual education plan and a 504 plan is for those who may not "qualify" for various reason for special education but need modifications for school in order for them to be more successful. These legal documents contain a lot of information about goals for the individual whether they are related to actual classroom things, school things, speech therapy, occupational therapy and physical therapy just to name a few. Goals are very important when you are working with any child but especially those in school.

What is my goal for Will? Well, a few years ago it was to get him to speak. We worked with various types of communication devices from a "talker" to a "PECS" book, picture exchange system, to different apps on the iPad. If you will remember the doctors told me that he would never speak, but I was set on proving them wrong. The English language is a very hard language to master. When you have some developmental delays, it becomes even more difficult. This is a verbal and social world that we live in, and to be able to function well you have to have communication abilities!

As we have made progress down the speech road the "goal" has shifted. Before I really had a good understanding of the world we live in, it was a very hard thing to grasp as to what the real goals should be. The real goal for Will is to be a functional member of society one day. As with any child, we as parents want them to have the best that they can possibly have in this life, and we want to do everything we can in order to help them attain those things. Often times, however, in our pursuit of those goals we lose sight of the "down the road" things because we are so laser focused on trying to survive today or right now. If you are walking this road I know you just agreed with me on that! However, we have to do our best today with our eye on those things down the road. I often say in my trainings, speeches, or workshops that the goal is one day for our children to walk out the door and be a functional member of society. That is every child and not just a few.

In light of the statement mentioned above, we, as the people surrounding our children, have to remain focused on the goal not just the things coming into our view today. Our teachers, family members, friends, therapists and others who are part of our team need to be relied upon to help foster all of those things that one day will need to be called upon for our children to be able to function in the world. We cannot modify the world for our kids no matter what the circumstances are surrounding them. When they walk out the door of their school one day there are no modifications out there. There will be no IEP or 504. They will have to walk out the door one day and no longer be in school. Everything we do for them needs to be in preparation for that one day. It is not humanly possible, nor should we expect the world to come all the way to them, we must take them towards the world in an effort to bring the world back towards them as well. It is a large task for sure but one well worth the effort on everyone's part.

We cannot do it alone nor should we continue to attempt to do so. No one is an island, and without the help of those around us we cannot make this a better place for any of our kids. God put people in our paths for a reason. Sometimes those reasons are for us and sometimes they are for others. I am very grateful for all those He has put in our path for either reason. They are many and continue to grow by the day.

What is the goal? Why are we doing exactly what we are doing? The goal is to give Will and all the other kids an opportunity to be a functional member of society. What will that actually look like? I really have no idea yet, but that will not keep me from walking or running towards it to help him. As I do that, we are also paving the road for many who are traveling it now and for those who are yet to get on it. The road will get a little bumpy, but hopefully not as much for the generation ahead of us.

Sometimes it is truly hard to see the forest for the trees, but we must stop long enough to do it for our kids and those in our communities. I want to challenge everyone who reads these words to examine yourself and the world around you, and try and figure out exactly why you do what you do. It may surprise you to see what is actually in the mirror when you do. You may need to stay the course or it might be time to change the course. You have a purpose in this world, everyone does, including your kids. If you will not fulfill your purpose, then please do not keep them from fulfilling why they are here. Time will only tell the direction we chose. What will you leave behind? Who will you leave behind? How will you leave them behind? Was the world a better place than when you found it, or have we done anything towards a better world for our kids?

CH14 AN OPEN LETTER

What's up big boy? I am not really sure when you will read this or understand everything I am going to tell you in here. There is a lot I want you to always know, remember, and so much I want to do and show you! I am sure I will leave something out because you know how I am and there is so much to say and do. I hope you always know I love you beyond what I could ever say and show you. I am really proud

of you and the man you are becoming! I hope you can always look at this and find peace and comfort for the road ahead of you..............

1: You have autism but autism doesn't have you. Brandi and I have fought for you for years concerning this, paving the road for you and so many others along this walk. There were a lot of times you couldn't communicate very well, but you are making great strides every day. We cannot wait to be able to tell you to be quiet one day! Keep fighting because we win!

2: You will never be allowed to use autism as an excuse for not doing the right things. You have

123

autism, but we will fight for all our days to not let autism have you! Many people have things that they deal with daily, and as you get older you will understand that more. There is an old saying that you always must remember, "There is no victory without the battle!" Battle on because we win!

3: For a long time, I felt sorry for you, me, and all those around us. What I didn't realize is that you are the greatest teacher I have ever had in my life. You don't care about all the junk in the world. You just want to know if people care about you. You are very special in so many ways, and I am honored and blessed to be your daddy because we win!

4: You will face many challenges in your life because as of now, the world doesn't see who we see in you. It is a cruel place out there, but there are still lots of great people that God has placed in our paths and will continue to do so. Always keep the attitude that you have and care for others! You have a great heart, and I pray you always do. Guess what? We win!

5: Always stand for right! You have a long heritage of it and I expect you to keep it going. Your last name does mean something, and your first name we have said for years was "God's Will", not just Will. Love the unlovable and help everyone you can because that is the heart God gave you! What will it look like..... Winners!

6: Be strong because you will need your strength to make your life the best it can be. The road will not be easy, but the rewards are priceless for Winners!

7: Always love and kiss your momma! She has basically given up her life for your success. She loves you very much and will always want to see you and get a kiss on the head from you. She is a huge part of why you are reading this many times throughout your life. She pushed me and you for a long time to get here. She is a winner and that gets us the outcome of... We Win!

8: This world is full of pain, and you are going to hurt people, and they will hurt you. Always forgive them, and always apologize to those you hurt. You have a great sense of reality of how people feel about you. They will know if you are sincere or not. We win!

9: Only trust people who have earned it. Many mistakes in this life could be avoided with those words. Not everyone has your best interest at heart, and with your sense of character you will know. Try to learn to look people in the eye and listen to your senses. You have a keen sense about people and trust that. I have always believed that was the Spirit living within you, speaking to you. We Win!

10: You may have to choose between successes and what's right.....always choose right. You have a last name to uphold on this Earth and a Father in Heaven who accepts nothing less than right. Right is not always popular, but We Win!

11: You will have many acquaintances but very few real friends. We Win!

12: Always strive to do what you love. You have great abilities and you need to utilize them. Someone will see your value, and you always hold your head high because We Win!

13: Be very sincere and humble. Life can be very cruel to anyone. You can teach many how to make it and have success when many thought differently! We Win!

14: Talk to God every day, all day long. He is always there for you. ALWAYS! He is the reason We Win!

15: Always know that daddy loves you beyond what you will ever know. I Win!

16: You are my hero, brother! You have fought the good fight and stayed the course. You hold your head high and love others. You be the example for others to follow. We Win!

17: Don't ever give up. Just when you think it is over, God says, "Not yet, My son! Remember always, WE WIN!

Daddy

DEDICATION

To everyone who I have ever come in contact with through various ways, I want to dedicate this book to you. I have been down in the depths of my existence at times and have also traveled to several mountain tops and there you were. Words cannot express the debt I owe God for placing each of you in my life.

INFORMATION

To contact Kris or Brandi Shinn about their business

Above All Else Inc
PO Box 692
Greenbrier, AR 72058
501-679-5677

www.aboveallelseservices.com
kris@aboveallelseservices.com